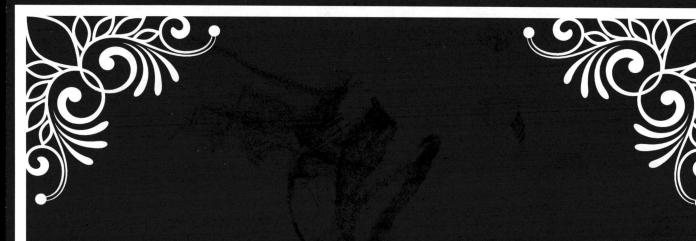

Payroll Ledger
Record Logbook

This Book Belongs To

NAME	ADDRESS

PHONE NUMBER	FAX

EMAIL

Book Info

BOOK START DATE	BOOK END DATE

BOOK NUMBER

Payroll Ledger

	Date	Page #
		1

Employee Name	Check Date	Check No.	Gross Pay	Total Deductions	Net Pay	Taxes With held

Payroll Ledger

	Date	Page #
		2

Employee Name	Check Date	Check No.	Gross Pay	Total Deductions	Net Pay	Taxes With held

Payroll Ledger

Date	Page #
	3

Employee Name	Check Date	Check No.	Gross Pay	Total Deductions	Net Pay	Taxes With held

Payroll Ledger

	Date	Page #
		4

Employee Name	Check Date	Check No.	Gross Pay	Total Deductions	Net Pay	Taxes With held

Payroll Ledger

Date	Page #
	5

Employee Name	Check Date	Check No.	Gross Pay	Total Deductions	Net Pay	Taxes With held

Payroll Ledger

	Date	Page #
		6

Employee Name	Check Date	Check No.	Gross Pay	Total Deductions	Net Pay	Taxes With held

Employee Name	Check Date	Check No.	Gross Pay	Total Deductions	Net Pay	Taxes With held

Payroll Ledger

Employee Name	Check Date	Check No.	Gross Pay	Total Deductions	Net Pay	Taxes With held

	Date				Page #	
					9	

Employee Name	Check Date	Check No.	Gross Pay	Total Deductions	Net Pay	Taxes With held

	Date				Page #
					10

Employee Name	Check Date	Check No.	Gross Pay	Total Deductions	Net Pay	Taxes With held

Payroll Ledger

Date	Page #
	11

Employee Name	Check Date	Check No.	Gross Pay	Total Deductions	Net Pay	Taxes With held

Payroll Ledger

	Date	Page #
		12

Employee Name	Check Date	Check No.	Gross Pay	Total Deductions	Net Pay	Taxes With held

Payroll Ledger

	Date	Page #
		13

Employee Name	Check Date	Check No.	Gross Pay	Total Deductions	Net Pay	Taxes With held

Payroll Ledger

	Date	Page #
		14

Employee Name	Check Date	Check No.	Gross Pay	Total Deductions	Net Pay	Taxes With held

Payroll Ledger

	Date	Page #
		15

Employee Name	Check Date	Check No.	Gross Pay	Total Deductions	Net Pay	Taxes With held

Payroll Ledger

	Date	Page #
		16

Employee Name	Check Date	Check No.	Gross Pay	Total Deductions	Net Pay	Taxes With held

Payroll Ledger

Date	Page #
	17

Employee Name	Check Date	Check No.	Gross Pay	Total Deductions	Net Pay	Taxes With held

Payroll Ledger

	Date	Page #
		18

Employee Name	Check Date	Check No.	Gross Pay	Total Deductions	Net Pay	Taxes With held

Payroll Ledger

	Date					Page #
						19

Employee Name	Check Date	Check No.	Gross Pay	Total Deductions	Net Pay	Taxes With held

Payroll Ledger

	Date	Page #
		20

Employee Name	Check Date	Check No.	Gross Pay	Total Deductions	Net Pay	Taxes With held

Payroll Ledger

	Date	Page #
		21

Employee Name	Check Date	Check No.	Gross Pay	Total Deductions	Net Pay	Taxes With held

Payroll Ledger

Employee Name	Check Date	Check No.	Gross Pay	Total Deductions	Net Pay	Taxes With held

Payroll Ledger

Employee Name	Check Date	Check No.	Gross Pay	Total Deductions	Net Pay	Taxes With held

Payroll Ledger

Employee Name	Check Date	Check No.	Gross Pay	Total Deductions	Net Pay	Taxes With held

Employee Name	Check Date	Check No.	Gross Pay	Total Deductions	Net Pay	Taxes With held

Payroll Ledger

	Date	Page #
		26

Employee Name	Check Date	Check No.	Gross Pay	Total Deductions	Net Pay	Taxes With held

Payroll Ledger

	Date	Page #
		27

Employee Name	Check Date	Check No.	Gross Pay	Total Deductions	Net Pay	Taxes With held

Employee Name	Check Date	Check No.	Gross Pay	Total Deductions	Net Pay	Taxes With held

Payroll Ledger

Employee Name	Check Date	Check No.	Gross Pay	Total Deductions	Net Pay	Taxes With held

Payroll Ledger

Employee Name	Check Date	Check No.	Gross Pay	Total Deductions	Net Pay	Taxes With held

Payroll Ledger

Employee Name	Check Date	Check No.	Gross Pay	Total Deductions	Net Pay	Taxes With held

Payroll Ledger

Employee Name	Check Date	Check No.	Gross Pay	Total Deductions	Net Pay	Taxes With held

Payroll Ledger

	Date	Page #
		33

Employee Name	Check Date	Check No.	Gross Pay	Total Deductions	Net Pay	Taxes With held

Payroll Ledger

Employee Name	Check Date	Check No.	Gross Pay	Total Deductions	Net Pay	Taxes With held

Payroll Ledger

	Date				Page #	
					35	

Employee Name	Check Date	Check No.	Gross Pay	Total Deductions	Net Pay	Taxes With held

Payroll Ledger

	Date	Page #
		36

Employee Name	Check Date	Check No.	Gross Pay	Total Deductions	Net Pay	Taxes With held

Payroll Ledger

	Date	Page #
		37

Employee Name	Check Date	Check No.	Gross Pay	Total Deductions	Net Pay	Taxes With held

Payroll Ledger

Employee Name	Check Date	Check No.	Gross Pay	Total Deductions	Net Pay	Taxes With held

Payroll Ledger

	Date	Page #
		39

Employee Name	Check Date	Check No.	Gross Pay	Total Deductions	Net Pay	Taxes With held

Payroll Ledger

Date	Page #
	40

Employee Name	Check Date	Check No.	Gross Pay	Total Deductions	Net Pay	Taxes With held

Payroll Ledger

	Date		Page #
			41

Employee Name	Check Date	Check No.	Gross Pay	Total Deductions	Net Pay	Taxes With held

Payroll Ledger

	Date	Page #
		42

Employee Name	Check Date	Check No.	Gross Pay	Total Deductions	Net Pay	Taxes With held

	Date				Page #
					43

Employee Name	Check Date	Check No.	Gross Pay	Total Deductions	Net Pay	Taxes With held

Payroll Ledger

	Date	Page #
		44

Employee Name	Check Date	Check No.	Gross Pay	Total Deductions	Net Pay	Taxes With held

Employee Name	Check Date	Check No.	Gross Pay	Total Deductions	Net Pay	Taxes With held

Payroll Ledger

	Date	Page #
		46

Employee Name	Check Date	Check No.	Gross Pay	Total Deductions	Net Pay	Taxes With held

Payroll Ledger

	Date	Page #
		47

Employee Name	Check Date	Check No.	Gross Pay	Total Deductions	Net Pay	Taxes With held

Payroll Ledger

	Date	Page #
		48

Employee Name	Check Date	Check No.	Gross Pay	Total Deductions	Net Pay	Taxes With held

Payroll Ledger

	Date	Page #
		49

Employee Name	Check Date	Check No.	Gross Pay	Total Deductions	Net Pay	Taxes With held

Payroll Ledger

	Date	Page #
		50

Employee Name	Check Date	Check No.	Gross Pay	Total Deductions	Net Pay	Taxes With held

Date					Page #	
					51	

Employee Name	Check Date	Check No.	Gross Pay	Total Deductions	Net Pay	Taxes With held

Payroll Ledger

	Date	Page #
		52

Employee Name	Check Date	Check No.	Gross Pay	Total Deductions	Net Pay	Taxes With held

Payroll Ledger

Employee Name	Check Date	Check No.	Gross Pay	Total Deductions	Net Pay	Taxes With held

Payroll Ledger

Employee Name	Check Date	Check No.	Gross Pay	Total Deductions	Net Pay	Taxes With held

Payroll Ledger

	Date	Page #
		55

Employee Name	Check Date	Check No.	Gross Pay	Total Deductions	Net Pay	Taxes With held

Payroll Ledger

	Date	Page #
		56

Employee Name	Check Date	Check No.	Gross Pay	Total Deductions	Net Pay	Taxes With held

Payroll Ledger

	Date				Page #
					57

Employee Name	Check Date	Check No.	Gross Pay	Total Deductions	Net Pay	Taxes With held

Payroll Ledger

	Date	Page #
		58

Employee Name	Check Date	Check No.	Gross Pay	Total Deductions	Net Pay	Taxes With held

Payroll Ledger

	Date	Page #
		59

Employee Name	Check Date	Check No.	Gross Pay	Total Deductions	Net Pay	Taxes With held

Payroll Ledger

Date	Page #
	60

Employee Name	Check Date	Check No.	Gross Pay	Total Deductions	Net Pay	Taxes With held

Payroll Ledger

Date		Page #
		61

Employee Name	Check Date	Check No.	Gross Pay	Total Deductions	Net Pay	Taxes With held

Employee Name	Check Date	Check No.	Gross Pay	Total Deductions	Net Pay	Taxes With held

Payroll Ledger

Employee Name	Check Date	Check No.	Gross Pay	Total Deductions	Net Pay	Taxes With held

Payroll Ledger

Employee Name	Check Date	Check No.	Gross Pay	Total Deductions	Net Pay	Taxes With held

Payroll Ledger

	Date	Page #
		65

Employee Name	Check Date	Check No.	Gross Pay	Total Deductions	Net Pay	Taxes With held

Payroll Ledger

	Date	Page #
		66

Employee Name	Check Date	Check No.	Gross Pay	Total Deductions	Net Pay	Taxes With held

Payroll Ledger

	Date	Page #
		67

Employee Name	Check Date	Check No.	Gross Pay	Total Deductions	Net Pay	Taxes With held

Employee Name	Check Date	Check No.	Gross Pay	Total Deductions	Net Pay	Taxes With held

Payroll Ledger

	Date	Page #
		69

Employee Name	Check Date	Check No.	Gross Pay	Total Deductions	Net Pay	Taxes With held

Payroll Ledger

Employee Name	Check Date	Check No.	Gross Pay	Total Deductions	Net Pay	Taxes With held

Payroll Ledger

Employee Name	Check Date	Check No.	Gross Pay	Total Deductions	Net Pay	Taxes With held

Payroll Ledger

	Date				Page #
					72

Employee Name	Check Date	Check No.	Gross Pay	Total Deductions	Net Pay	Taxes With held

Payroll Ledger

Date		Page #
		73

Employee Name	Check Date	Check No.	Gross Pay	Total Deductions	Net Pay	Taxes With held

Payroll Ledger

Date	Page #
	74

Employee Name	Check Date	Check No.	Gross Pay	Total Deductions	Net Pay	Taxes With held

Payroll Ledger

Employee Name	Check Date	Check No.	Gross Pay	Total Deductions	Net Pay	Taxes With held

Payroll Ledger

	Date	Page #
		76

Employee Name	Check Date	Check No.	Gross Pay	Total Deductions	Net Pay	Taxes With held

Payroll Ledger

	Date	Page #
		77

Employee Name	Check Date	Check No.	Gross Pay	Total Deductions	Net Pay	Taxes With held

Payroll Ledger

Employee Name	Check Date	Check No.	Gross Pay	Total Deductions	Net Pay	Taxes With held

Payroll Ledger

	Date	Page #
		79

Employee Name	Check Date	Check No.	Gross Pay	Total Deductions	Net Pay	Taxes With held

Payroll Ledger

Employee Name	Check Date	Check No.	Gross Pay	Total Deductions	Net Pay	Taxes With held

Payroll Ledger

	Date	Page #
		81

Employee Name	Check Date	Check No.	Gross Pay	Total Deductions	Net Pay	Taxes With held
.						

Payroll Ledger

	Date	Page #
		82

Employee Name	Check Date	Check No.	Gross Pay	Total Deductions	Net Pay	Taxes With held

Payroll Ledger

Date	Page #
	83

Employee Name	Check Date	Check No.	Gross Pay	Total Deductions	Net Pay	Taxes With held

Employee Name	Check Date	Check No.	Gross Pay	Total Deductions	Net Pay	Taxes With held

Payroll Ledger

Date	Page #
	85

Employee Name	Check Date	Check No.	Gross Pay	Total Deductions	Net Pay	Taxes With held

Payroll Ledger

	Date				Page #	
					86	

Employee Name	Check Date	Check No.	Gross Pay	Total Deductions	Net Pay	Taxes With held

Payroll Ledger

	Date	Page #
		87

Employee Name	Check Date	Check No.	Gross Pay	Total Deductions	Net Pay	Taxes With held

Payroll Ledger

	Date	Page #
		88

Employee Name	Check Date	Check No.	Gross Pay	Total Deductions	Net Pay	Taxes With held

Payroll Ledger

	Date	Page #
		89

Employee Name	Check Date	Check No.	Gross Pay	Total Deductions	Net Pay	Taxes With held

Payroll Ledger

Employee Name	Check Date	Check No.	Gross Pay	Total Deductions	Net Pay	Taxes With held

Payroll Ledger

	Date	Page #
		91

Employee Name	Check Date	Check No.	Gross Pay	Total Deductions	Net Pay	Taxes With held

Payroll Ledger

Employee Name	Check Date	Check No.	Gross Pay	Total Deductions	Net Pay	Taxes With held

Payroll Ledger

	Date	Page #
		93

Employee Name	Check Date	Check No.	Gross Pay	Total Deductions	Net Pay	Taxes With held

Payroll Ledger

	Date	Page #
		94

Employee Name	Check Date	Check No.	Gross Pay	Total Deductions	Net Pay	Taxes With held

Payroll Ledger

	Date				Page #
					95

Employee Name	Check Date	Check No.	Gross Pay	Total Deductions	Net Pay	Taxes With held

Payroll Ledger

Employee Name	Check Date	Check No.	Gross Pay	Total Deductions	Net Pay	Taxes With held

Payroll Ledger

	Date				Page #
					97

Employee Name	Check Date	Check No.	Gross Pay	Total Deductions	Net Pay	Taxes With held

Payroll Ledger

Date	Page #
	98

Employee Name	Check Date	Check No.	Gross Pay	Total Deductions	Net Pay	Taxes With held

Payroll Ledger

	Date	Page #
		99

Employee Name	Check Date	Check No.	Gross Pay	Total Deductions	Net Pay	Taxes With held

Payroll Ledger

	Date					Page #
						100

Employee Name	Check Date	Check No.	Gross Pay	Total Deductions	Net Pay	Taxes With held

Payroll Ledger

	Date		Page #
			101

Employee Name	Check Date	Check No.	Gross Pay	Total Deductions	Net Pay	Taxes With held

Payroll Ledger

	Date	Page #
		102

Employee Name	Check Date	Check No.	Gross Pay	Total Deductions	Net Pay	Taxes With held

Payroll Ledger

Date	Page #
	103

Employee Name	Check Date	Check No.	Gross Pay	Total Deductions	Net Pay	Taxes With held

Payroll Ledger

	Date	Page #
		104

Employee Name	Check Date	Check No.	Gross Pay	Total Deductions	Net Pay	Taxes With held

Payroll Ledger

Date	Page #
	105

Employee Name	Check Date	Check No.	Gross Pay	Total Deductions	Net Pay	Taxes With held

Employee Name	Check Date	Check No.	Gross Pay	Total Deductions	Net Pay	Taxes With held

Payroll Ledger

Employee Name	Check Date	Check No.	Gross Pay	Total Deductions	Net Pay	Taxes With held

Payroll Ledger

	Date				Page #
					108

Employee Name	Check Date	Check No.	Gross Pay	Total Deductions	Net Pay	Taxes With held

Made in the USA
Columbia, SC
22 August 2022

65852637R00061